The Ultimate Guide to Subscription Boxes Discovering the Perfect Monthly Treats for Busy Employees

Shepherd Saul

Copyright © [2023]

**Title: The Ultimate Guide to Subscription Boxes Discovering the Perfect Monthly Treats for Busy Employees
Author's: Shepherd Saul**

This book was printed and published by [Publisher's: **Shepherd Saul**] in [2023]

ISBN:

TABLE OF CONTENT

Chapter 3: Popular Subscription Box Niches for Busy Employees   22

Chapter 4: How to Get the Most Out of Your Subscription Box   36

Chapter 5: Managing Your Subscription Box Subscriptions 46

Chapter 6: Exploring Subscription Box Alternatives 56

Chapter 7: Subscription Box Etiquette and Best Practices

Chapter 9: Conclusion: Finding Your Perfect Monthly Treat 86

Reflecting on Your Subscription Box Journey

Continuing to Explore and Discover New Subscription Boxes

Embracing the Joy of Monthly Surprises

Chapter 1: Introduction to Subscription Boxes

What are Subscription Boxes?

In this digital age, where convenience and personalized experiences reign supreme, subscription boxes have emerged as a popular trend in the e-commerce industry. If you're an employee looking to add a touch of excitement to your busy life, subscription boxes might just be the perfect solution for you.

So, what exactly are subscription boxes? Simply put, they are a curated selection of products that are delivered to your doorstep on a monthly basis. These boxes are tailored to cater to various interests, hobbies, and needs, making them a delightful surprise every time they arrive.

Subscription boxes come in all shapes and sizes, catering to a wide range of niches and preferences. Whether you're a fashionista, a fitness enthusiast, a food connoisseur, or a bookworm, there's a subscription box out there that is tailored specifically for you. These boxes can include anything from clothing and accessories, to beauty products, gourmet snacks, wellness items, books, and so much more. The possibilities are endless!

One of the greatest benefits of subscription boxes is the element of surprise they bring into your life. Imagine the anticipation and excitement of receiving a beautifully packaged box every month, not knowing what treasures lie within. It's like receiving a gift from yourself to yourself, and who doesn't love that?

Subscription boxes also offer convenience, especially for busy employees. With a simple subscription, you can have your monthly treats delivered right to your doorstep without having to spend precious time shopping or researching for new products. It's like having a personal shopper who understands your preferences and curates a selection just for you.

Moreover, subscription boxes provide an opportunity to discover new brands and products that you may not have come across otherwise. Many of these boxes feature small, independent businesses that offer unique and high-quality products. By subscribing to these boxes, you not only support these smaller brands but also get to experience their products firsthand.

In conclusion, subscription boxes have revolutionized the way we shop and indulge ourselves. They offer convenience, excitement, and discovery, making them the perfect monthly treat for busy employees like you. So, why not treat yourself to a subscription box and add a little joy and surprise to your life? You deserve it!

The Rise of Subscription Box Businesses

In recent years, there has been a remarkable surge in the popularity of subscription box businesses. Through the convenience of online shopping, these businesses have revolutionized the way we discover and enjoy new products. With their curated packages delivered right to our doorsteps, subscription boxes have become a go-to solution for busy employees looking to treat themselves with a little monthly indulgence.

One of the key factors behind the rise of subscription box businesses is the convenience they offer. As employees with demanding schedules, finding the time to explore new products and brands can be challenging. Subscription boxes eliminate this problem by carefully selecting and curating a variety of items based on your preferences. Whether it's beauty products, gourmet snacks, or even books and games, there is a subscription box for every niche interest.

E-commerce has played a crucial role in the growth of subscription box businesses. With the increasing number of online shoppers, it has become easier for these businesses to reach a wider audience and cater to different niches. The online platform allows for easy customization, ensuring that employees receive products they genuinely enjoy. Moreover, the subscription model provides a seamless shopping experience, as employees only need to sign up once and then sit back and relax while their monthly treat is delivered to their doorstep.

Another reason for the rise in popularity of subscription boxes is the element of surprise they bring. Opening a subscription box creates a sense of anticipation and excitement, akin to unwrapping a gift. This surprise factor adds an extra layer of joy to the shopping experience, making it all the more enjoyable for busy employees who deserve a little pampering.

Subscription box businesses have also become a powerful marketing tool for brands. By partnering with subscription box companies, brands can introduce their products to a targeted audience. This allows for greater exposure and a chance to build brand loyalty. Employees can discover new products and brands they may have never come across otherwise, enabling them to make informed purchasing decisions in the future.

In conclusion, the rise of subscription box businesses has transformed the way busy employees shop for and experience new products. Through their convenience, customization, surprise factor, and marketing partnerships, subscription boxes have become an increasingly popular choice in the e-commerce world. So why not treat yourself to a monthly surprise and indulge in the ultimate shopping experience delivered right to your doorstep?

Benefits of Subscription Boxes for Busy Employees

In today's fast-paced world, where time is a precious commodity, finding ways to simplify our lives and make things more convenient is paramount. As busy employees, juggling work responsibilities, personal commitments, and maintaining a healthy work-life balance can often feel overwhelming. This is where subscription boxes come in as a game-changer for busy professionals like you. In this subchapter, we will explore the numerous benefits of subscription boxes tailored specifically for busy employees in the e-commerce industry.

1. Time-Saving Convenience: With subscription boxes, the hassle of researching, shopping, and trying to find the perfect products is eliminated. These boxes are carefully curated with items that are handpicked to suit your needs and preferences. By subscribing to a monthly box, you save valuable time that would otherwise be spent searching and shopping for various products.

2. Personalized Selections: Subscription boxes often allow you to customize your preferences, ensuring that you receive products that align with your personal tastes and lifestyle. Whether it's beauty and grooming products, healthy snacks, or office essentials, these boxes cater to your individual needs, making each delivery a delightful surprise.

3. Discover New Products: Subscription boxes offer an excellent opportunity to explore and discover new products that you may not have otherwise stumbled upon. These boxes often include samples or full-sized products from both established and emerging brands. By trying out new products, you can expand your horizons and find hidden gems that enhance your daily routine.

4. Boosting Morale and Well-being: As a busy employee, it's essential to prioritize self-care and well-being. Subscription boxes often include items that promote relaxation, stress relief, and overall wellness. From aromatherapy products to mindfulness tools, these boxes provide a monthly treat that helps you unwind and rejuvenate after a long day at work.

5. Cost-Effective: Subscription boxes are not only convenient but can also be cost-effective. Many boxes offer a significant discount compared to purchasing each item individually. This allows you to enjoy high-quality products without breaking the bank. Additionally, by receiving products regularly, you can better manage your budget and avoid impulsive purchases.

In conclusion, subscription boxes are a game-changer for busy employees in the e-commerce industry. With their time-saving convenience, personalized selections, and the opportunity to discover new products, these boxes enhance your daily routine while promoting self-care and well-being. So, why not treat yourself to a subscription box and experience the joy of receiving a monthly surprise tailored just for you?

Chapter 2: Choosing the Right Subscription Box

Identifying Your Interests and Needs

In the fast-paced world of e-commerce, where time is often a luxury, it's crucial for busy employees to find ways to unwind and treat themselves. Subscription boxes have emerged as a popular solution, providing a monthly dose of joy and relaxation delivered straight to your doorstep. However, with the vast array of options available, it can be overwhelming to determine which subscription box is the perfect fit for your specific interests and needs. This subchapter aims to guide employees in identifying their unique preferences, ensuring they discover the ultimate subscription box experience tailored to their individual tastes.

Before diving into the wide selection of subscription boxes, take a moment to reflect on your interests and hobbies. Are you a foodie who enjoys exploring new flavors? Perhaps you're a bookworm seeking literary adventures? Or maybe you're a beauty enthusiast who loves experimenting with skincare and makeup products? Identifying your passions will help narrow down the vast array of subscription boxes available, ensuring you find one that aligns with your specific interests.

Additionally, it's essential to consider your needs when selecting a subscription box. Are you looking for products that promote self-care and relaxation, providing a much-needed escape from your hectic work schedule? Or do you prefer boxes that offer practical items to enhance your productivity and organization? By understanding your needs, you can prioritize finding a subscription box that caters to your requirements, helping you strike the perfect balance between work and personal life.

Another critical factor to consider is your budget. Subscription boxes come in various price ranges, and it's crucial to determine how much you're willing to invest in this monthly treat. Assess your financial situation and set a budget that aligns with your priorities, ensuring you find a subscription box that not only fits your interests but also your wallet.

Lastly, don't forget to read reviews and explore different subscription box options. Researching various providers will give you an idea of the quality, variety, and overall value they offer. Look for testimonials from other employees who share similar interests and needs, as their experiences can provide valuable insights to help inform your decision.

By taking the time to identify your interests, needs, and budget while conducting thorough research, you can confidently select a subscription box that will enhance your overall well-being, provide a monthly treat to look forward to, and ultimately make your busy employee life a little brighter.

Researching Different Subscription Box Niches

In today's fast-paced world, it can be challenging for busy employees to find the time to indulge in self-care or discover new products that enhance their lives. This is where subscription boxes come in. Subscription boxes offer a convenient and exciting way to receive curated products delivered straight to your doorstep on a monthly basis. With the rise of e-commerce, there is a wealth of subscription box niches to explore, catering to a wide range of interests and needs. In this subchapter, we will delve into the importance of researching different subscription box niches, particularly within the realm of e-commerce.

When it comes to choosing the perfect subscription box, research is key. There are countless options out there, each tailored to specific interests, hobbies, and lifestyles. By taking the time to research different niches, employees can find a subscription box that aligns with their passions and preferences, ensuring they receive a monthly treat that truly excites them.

One of the most popular subscription box niches within the e-commerce industry is beauty and skincare. These boxes often feature a variety of carefully selected products, including skincare essentials, makeup items, and beauty tools. Researching different beauty and skincare subscription boxes allows employees to discover new brands, test out products before committing to full-sized versions, and stay up-to-date with the latest trends in the industry.

For those with a passion for health and wellness, there are subscription boxes that focus on providing organic snacks, fitness gear, and wellness products. Exploring different options in this niche can help employees discover new ways to prioritize their well-being and maintain a healthy lifestyle.

Another niche worth exploring is the food and cooking subscription box market. From gourmet ingredients and meal kits to unique snacks and beverages, these boxes offer employees the opportunity to experience new flavors and expand their culinary horizons. By researching different food and cooking subscription box options, employees can find one that matches their dietary preferences, whether they are vegetarian, vegan, or have specific allergies.

In conclusion, researching different subscription box niches within the e-commerce industry is essential for busy employees who wish to enhance their lives and treat themselves to monthly surprises. Whether it's beauty and skincare, health and wellness, or food and cooking, taking the time to explore various options ensures that employees find a subscription box that caters to their specific interests, bringing joy and convenience to their busy lives.

Reading Reviews and Recommendations

In today's digital age, reading reviews and recommendations has become an essential step in making informed purchasing decisions. This holds true, especially in the world of e-commerce and subscription boxes. As busy employees, you want to ensure that you are investing your hard-earned money in the perfect monthly treats that will bring joy and excitement to your life. That's why this chapter is dedicated to guiding you through the process of reading reviews and recommendations to help you discover the ultimate subscription box that suits your preferences.

Online reviews have revolutionized the way we shop. They provide valuable insights from real customers who have already experienced the products or services you are considering. When it comes to subscription boxes, reading reviews can be particularly helpful since they offer a glimpse into the variety, quality, and overall value that a particular box delivers. By delving into the experiences of others, you can gain a better understanding of whether a specific subscription box aligns with your interests and needs.

One of the most reliable sources of reviews and recommendations is online platforms dedicated to subscription box enthusiasts. These platforms bring together a community of like-minded individuals who share their unfiltered opinions and experiences. By actively participating in these forums, you can ask questions, seek advice, and receive personalized recommendations from fellow employees who have similar interests. This allows you to tap into a wealth of knowledge and make well-informed decisions.

Additionally, social media has become a powerful tool for discovering subscription box trends and recommendations. Follow influencers and bloggers who specialize in reviewing subscription boxes within your niche. Their honest and detailed feedback, often accompanied by captivating visuals, can give you a better idea of what to expect from different boxes. Engaging with these influencers and their followers can also provide you with a platform to discuss your preferences and receive personalized recommendations.

However, it is important to approach reviews with a critical eye. While they can provide valuable insights, remember that everyone's preferences and expectations may vary. It is crucial to consider the overall consensus and weigh multiple reviews to form a well-rounded opinion. Always prioritize reviews from trusted sources and be open to trying new subscription boxes that align with your interests, even if they don't have a plethora of reviews.

In conclusion, reading reviews and recommendations is an essential step in finding the perfect monthly treat through subscription boxes. By leveraging the power of online platforms, social media, and engaging with influencers, you can gain valuable insights and personalized recommendations. Remember to approach reviews with a critical mindset and be open to exploring new options. Happy reading and discovering your ideal subscription box!

Considering Pricing and Value for Money

One of the key aspects to keep in mind when delving into the world of subscription boxes is pricing and value for money. As employees who are interested in exploring the realm of e-commerce, it is crucial to understand the significance of these factors in order to make informed decisions and get the most out of your monthly treats.

When it comes to pricing, it is important to remember that subscription boxes vary greatly in terms of cost. Some may be more budget-friendly, while others may be on the higher end. It is essential to assess your financial situation and determine a realistic budget for your subscription box indulgence. Consider asking yourself questions such as, "How much am I willing to spend monthly on a subscription box?" and "What value am I expecting to receive in return?"

Value for money is an equally important aspect to consider. While the price may be within your budget, it is crucial to evaluate whether the contents of the box align with your expectations and preferences. Take the time to research and read reviews from fellow subscribers to gain insights into the quality and variety of items typically included. This will help you determine if the subscription box offers genuine value for your hard-earned money.

Additionally, it is worth considering the overall experience and convenience that a subscription box provides. Does it offer customization options based on your preferences? Does it provide an enjoyable unboxing experience? Does it save you time by curating products that you would have otherwise spent hours searching for online? These factors contribute to the overall value you receive from your subscription box.

Remember, subscribing to a box that offers the perfect balance between pricing and value for money can enhance your overall shopping experience. It provides you with an opportunity to discover new products, indulge in self-care, and enjoy the element of surprise every month.

In conclusion, as employees with an interest in e-commerce, it is crucial to carefully consider pricing and value for money when exploring subscription boxes. By setting a realistic budget, evaluating the contents and overall experience, and reading reviews, you can ensure that you are getting the most out of your subscription box treats. So go ahead, embark on this delightful journey and discover the perfect monthly treats for yourself!

Chapter 3: Popular Subscription Box Niches for Busy Employees

Beauty and Skincare Subscription Boxes

In the world of e-commerce, subscription boxes have taken the market by storm. And one of the most popular niches within this industry is beauty and skincare subscription boxes. These boxes offer employees a convenient and exciting way to discover new beauty products and pamper themselves without the hassle of researching and shopping for individual items.

Beauty and skincare subscription boxes are curated by experts in the field who carefully select a variety of high-quality products from both well-known brands and emerging beauty companies. Each month, employees receive a box filled with deluxe samples or full-sized products, allowing them to try out different items and find what works best for their skin and beauty routine.

One of the key benefits of beauty and skincare subscription boxes is the element of surprise. Opening a box filled with carefully wrapped products is like receiving a monthly gift, creating a sense of anticipation and excitement. It's a perfect way for busy employees to treat themselves and indulge in some self-care, even in the midst of their hectic schedules.

These subscription boxes cater to employees of all skin types, ages, and beauty preferences. Whether someone is interested in organic and cruelty-free products, Korean skincare, or luxurious high-end brands, there is a subscription box that matches their needs. This wide range of options ensures that every employee can find the perfect box that aligns with their personal tastes and skincare goals.

Furthermore, beauty and skincare subscription boxes often come with additional perks. Many boxes include detailed product descriptions and usage instructions, helping employees make the most of each item they receive. Some subscription services also offer exclusive discounts and access to limited edition products, creating a sense of exclusivity for subscribers.

Subscribing to a beauty and skincare box is not only a convenient and enjoyable experience for employees, but it also supports the growth of small businesses and emerging beauty brands. By purchasing these boxes, employees contribute to the success of these companies, helping them gain exposure and reach a wider audience.

In conclusion, beauty and skincare subscription boxes are an excellent choice for employees looking to discover new beauty products, indulge in self-care, and simplify their beauty routine. With a wide variety of options available, these boxes offer something for everyone, making them a perfect addition to the e-commerce world. So why not treat yourself to a monthly surprise and elevate your beauty and skincare game with a subscription box?

Fitness and Wellness Subscription Boxes

In today's fast-paced world, maintaining a healthy lifestyle can be quite challenging, especially for busy employees. With long working hours and limited time for self-care, it's easy to neglect our physical and mental well-being. However, there is a solution that can help you prioritize your health without adding extra stress to your already hectic schedule - fitness and wellness subscription boxes.

Fitness and wellness subscription boxes are a game-changer in the world of E-commerce. These curated boxes are designed to provide you with a monthly dose of motivation, inspiration, and tools to support your fitness and wellness journey. Whether you are a fitness enthusiast or just starting your wellness transformation, these subscription boxes are tailored to meet your individual needs and goals.

Each month, you will receive a carefully selected assortment of products that encompass various aspects of fitness and wellness. From nutritious snacks and supplements to workout gear and self-care items, these boxes offer a holistic approach to well-being. They are like having a personal trainer, nutritionist, and wellness coach all rolled into one.

One of the greatest benefits of subscribing to these boxes is the convenience they offer. As an employee, time is of the essence, and finding the right products that align with your goals can be time-consuming. With fitness and wellness subscription boxes, all the research and product sourcing is done for you. You can simply sit back, relax, and enjoy the surprise of discovering new products that will enhance your fitness and wellness journey.

Moreover, these subscription boxes often come with expert guidance and resources. Many boxes include workout plans, nutrition tips, and access to online communities where you can connect with like-minded individuals. This additional support system ensures that you stay motivated and accountable, even when life gets busy.

Investing in your fitness and wellness not only improves your physical health but also boosts your mental well-being. By prioritizing self-care, you will have more energy, enhanced productivity, and an overall better quality of life. So, why not take advantage of the convenience and value offered by fitness and wellness subscription boxes?

In conclusion, as an employee in the E-commerce niche, it's crucial to find ways to prioritize your health and well-being. Fitness and wellness subscription boxes offer a convenient and effective solution to support your fitness goals and self-care routine. With carefully curated products, expert guidance, and a supportive community, these boxes are the perfect monthly treat for busy employees like you. Start your wellness transformation today and discover the benefits of these amazing subscription boxes.

Healthy Snack and Food Subscription Boxes

In today's fast-paced world, it can be challenging for employees to maintain a healthy diet and find the time to prepare nutritious meals. As a result, many turn to convenient options that are often laden with unhealthy ingredients. However, there is a solution that can make eating healthy easier and more enjoyable - Healthy Snack and Food Subscription Boxes.

These subscription boxes are a godsend for busy employees who are looking to improve their eating habits. They offer a wide variety of delicious and nutritious snacks and meals that are delivered straight to your doorstep every month. With just a few clicks, you can have a selection of wholesome treats at your fingertips, making it easier than ever to fuel your body with the nutrients it needs.

One of the most significant advantages of these subscription boxes is the convenience they provide. As an employee in the e-commerce industry, you likely have a demanding schedule that leaves little time for grocery shopping and meal prepping. With a healthy snack and food subscription box, you can say goodbye to those rushed trips to the grocery store and hello to hassle-free healthy eating. These boxes come packed with a curated selection of snacks and meals, making it easy to grab and go, whether you're heading to the office or working remotely.

Another benefit of these subscription boxes is the breadth of options available. Whether you're following a specific diet, such as vegan, gluten-free, or paleo, or simply looking for a variety of healthy snacks to keep you energized throughout the day, there is a subscription box out there for you. From protein bars and nut mixes to gourmet granolas and superfood smoothie kits, the choices are endless. Plus, many companies allow you to personalize your box based on your preferences and dietary restrictions.

Additionally, subscribing to a healthy snack and food box can be a cost-effective way to eat well. By eliminating impulsive snack purchases and reducing food waste, you can save money in the long run. Furthermore, some subscription box companies offer discounts and promotions for loyal customers, making it even more affordable to nourish your body with wholesome treats.

In conclusion, healthy snack and food subscription boxes are a game-changer for busy employees in the e-commerce industry. They provide convenience, variety, and cost savings, allowing you to effortlessly incorporate healthy eating into your busy lifestyle. So why not treat yourself to a monthly delivery of nutritious snacks and meals? Your body and mind will thank you for it!

Self-Care and Relaxation Subscription Boxes

In our fast-paced and demanding world, it's easy for employees to neglect their own well-being. The constant pressure to meet deadlines, achieve targets, and juggle personal responsibilities can leave us feeling stressed, overwhelmed, and burnt out. That's where self-care and relaxation subscription boxes come in to offer a much-needed respite.

Subscribing to a self-care and relaxation subscription box is like giving yourself a monthly gift that promotes relaxation, rejuvenation, and overall well-being. These boxes are carefully curated with a range of products and activities designed to help you unwind, de-stress, and prioritize self-care. From luxurious bath and body products to mindfulness tools, these subscription boxes are the perfect way to treat yourself and make self-care a priority.

One of the great advantages of these boxes is the element of surprise they bring. Each month, you'll receive a thoughtfully curated selection of products that are tailored to help you relax and recharge. From aromatic candles and essential oils to calming teas and skincare products, these boxes provide a variety of items that cater to different self-care needs.

Moreover, self-care and relaxation subscription boxes offer a convenient and hassle-free way to prioritize your well-being. With just a few clicks, you can sign up for a subscription and have these boxes delivered right to your doorstep. This eliminates the need to spend time searching for self-care products and ensures that you always have a monthly treat to look forward to.

Additionally, these subscription boxes are an excellent way to explore new products and discover new self-care practices. With the diverse range of items included in each box, you'll have the opportunity to try out different relaxation techniques, explore new scents, and experiment with various self-care rituals. This not only enhances your well-being but also adds a sense of excitement and discovery to your self-care routine.

As employees in the e-commerce industry, we often find ourselves immersed in a digital world, constantly connected and always "on." Subscribing to a self-care and relaxation subscription box provides an opportunity to disconnect from the virtual realm and focus on our well-being. By dedicating time to prioritize self-care, we can recharge our batteries, improve our mental and physical health, and ultimately become more productive and fulfilled in our professional and personal lives.

In conclusion, self-care and relaxation subscription boxes offer a convenient, enjoyable, and effective way for busy employees in the e-commerce industry to prioritize their well-being. By subscribing to these monthly treats, we can nurture ourselves, reduce stress, and cultivate a healthier work-life balance. So go ahead, give yourself the gift of self-care and relaxation, and discover the perfect monthly treat that will help you thrive as an employee in the fast-paced world of e-commerce.

Professional Development and Productivity Subscription Boxes

In today's fast-paced world, staying ahead of the curve and continuously improving oneself has become more important than ever. As employees in the e-commerce industry, you understand the significance of professional development and productivity in order to thrive in your career. This subchapter will introduce you to the world of professional development and productivity subscription boxes, your key to unlocking your true potential and achieving your goals.

Professional development and productivity subscription boxes are carefully curated packages designed to provide you with the tools, resources, and inspiration needed to enhance your skills, boost productivity, and stay motivated. These boxes are tailored specifically for employees like you, who are dedicated to excelling in their careers and making a lasting impact in the e-commerce industry.

Each month, you can expect to receive a box filled with valuable resources such as books, online courses, webinars, and workshops, all focused on a specific area of professional development. Whether you want to improve your leadership skills, enhance your communication abilities, or learn the latest trends in e-commerce, there is a subscription box that caters to your specific needs.

Not only do these boxes provide you with the necessary tools for growth, but they also offer a unique opportunity to explore new ideas and connect with like-minded individuals. Many subscription boxes include access to exclusive online communities, where you can engage in discussions with experts and fellow subscribers, fostering a supportive network that encourages learning and collaboration.

By investing in a professional development and productivity subscription box, you are investing in yourself and your future. These boxes offer a convenient and cost-effective way to continuously learn and develop new skills, without the hassle of searching for resources or attending time-consuming workshops. With each box, you'll be one step closer to becoming the best version of yourself, both personally and professionally.

So why wait? Take control of your professional growth and productivity today by subscribing to a professional development and productivity subscription box. Prepare to be inspired, learn new skills, and unlock your full potential in the e-commerce industry. Your journey to success starts now!

Pet Supplies and Toys Subscription Boxes

For all the pet lovers out there who constantly find themselves running out of pet supplies or struggling to find new toys to keep their furry friends entertained, pet supplies and toys subscription boxes are the answer to your prayers. These subscription boxes are specifically curated for your pets, ensuring they receive the best quality products month after month. As a busy employee, you can now enjoy the convenience of having pet supplies and toys delivered right to your doorstep, saving you time and effort.

E-Commerce has revolutionized the way we shop, and pet supplies and toys are no exception. With the rise of online shopping, pet owners now have access to an incredible variety of products tailored to their pets' needs. However, navigating through countless options and trying to figure out what is best for your furry companion can be overwhelming. That's where pet supplies and toys subscription boxes come in.

By subscribing to a pet supplies and toys subscription box, you can say goodbye to the hassle of searching for the perfect products for your pets. These boxes are carefully curated by experts who understand the needs and preferences of different pets. Each month, you will receive a selection of high-quality pet supplies and toys, ensuring your furry friend is always well taken care of and entertained.

The convenience of these subscription boxes is unmatched. As an employee juggling multiple responsibilities, finding time to shop for pet supplies can be challenging. With a pet supplies and toys subscription box, you can eliminate the stress of running out of essential items for your pet. You no longer have to make last-minute trips to the store or spend hours browsing online. Instead, you can focus on your work and leave the task of providing for your pet to the experts.

Furthermore, these subscription boxes offer a fantastic opportunity for pet owners to discover new brands and products. Each box is carefully curated to include a variety of items, allowing you to try out different brands and see what works best for your pet. This eliminates the need for trial and error, saving you both time and money.

In conclusion, pet supplies and toys subscription boxes are a game-changer for busy employees who want to ensure their pets receive the best care and entertainment. With the convenience and expert curation offered by these boxes, you can provide for your pet without sacrificing precious time or energy. So why not treat yourself and your furry friend to a monthly subscription box and enjoy the benefits it brings to both you and your pet's lives?

Other Niche Subscription Boxes for Employees

In addition to the popular subscription boxes available for busy employees, such as wellness, beauty, and food, there are several other niche options that cater specifically to those working in the e-commerce industry. These unique subscription boxes are designed to provide valuable resources, tools, and products that can enhance productivity, creativity, and overall job satisfaction for e-commerce professionals. Here are some of the top niche subscription boxes for employees in the e-commerce industry.

1. Tech Gear Box: As an e-commerce employee, staying up to date with the latest technology trends is crucial. The Tech Gear Box subscription delivers cutting-edge gadgets, accessories, and software to help you stay ahead of the game. From portable chargers to productivity-boosting apps, this box is perfect for tech-savvy individuals looking to optimize their work environment.

2. Marketing Mastery Box: Marketing is a vital aspect of any successful e-commerce business. This subscription box is designed to help employees in the marketing department stay on top of the latest strategies and trends. Each month, you'll receive books, courses, and tools that can enhance your digital marketing skills and help you generate more traffic and sales for your online store.

3. Entrepreneur's Toolkit: For those ambitious employees dreaming of launching their own e-commerce ventures, the Entrepreneur's Toolkit subscription box is a must-have. This box includes resources, books, and online courses that will guide you through the process of starting and scaling your own business. From business planning to marketing strategies, this box will equip you with the knowledge and tools you need to succeed as an e-commerce entrepreneur.

4. Creative Inspiration Box: E-commerce professionals often need a dose of creativity to design engaging websites, captivating social media posts, and eye-catching graphics. The Creative Inspiration Box provides monthly doses of inspiration, including books, art supplies, and unique products that can spark your creativity and help you produce outstanding visual content for your e-commerce business.

5. Stress Relief Box: The e-commerce industry can be fast-paced and demanding, leading to high levels of stress among employees. The Stress Relief Box is designed to help you unwind and relax after a long day. Each month, you'll receive calming teas, aromatherapy products, stress balls, and other stress-relief tools that will help you recharge and maintain a healthy work-life balance.

These niche subscription boxes cater specifically to the needs of e-commerce employees, offering valuable resources, tools, and products that can enhance productivity, creativity, and overall job satisfaction. Consider subscribing to one or more of these boxes to enhance your e-commerce career and make your work life more enjoyable.

Chapter 4: How to Get the Most Out of Your Subscription Box

Unboxing and First Impressions

As employees in today's fast-paced world, we often find ourselves overwhelmed with work and the demands of our daily lives. That's why we deserve a treat, a little something to brighten our day and make us feel appreciated. Enter subscription boxes – the ultimate solution for busy employees seeking monthly surprises that are tailor-made just for them. In this subchapter, we will delve into the exciting world of unboxing and share our first impressions of these delightful packages, specifically curated for the e-commerce niche.

Unboxing a subscription box is like unwrapping a present, filled with anticipation and excitement. The moment it arrives at your doorstep, you can't help but feel a wave of delight. As you carefully open the package, each item is revealed, one by one, creating a sense of wonderment and curiosity. The well-designed packaging, often adorned with vibrant colors and personalized touches, adds an extra layer of joy to the experience.

The first impressions of a subscription box are crucial, and they rarely disappoint. From the moment you lay eyes on the contents, you can tell that the box has been carefully curated to cater to your specific interests and needs. Whether it's a box filled with gourmet snacks, trendy fashion accessories, or innovative gadgets, you can't help but appreciate the thought and effort that went into selecting each item.

The quality of the products within the box is of utmost importance. As busy employees, we don't have the time to search for the best and latest items in the market. Subscription boxes take care of that for us, ensuring that we receive high-quality products that are both useful and enjoyable. This initial impression sets the tone for our ongoing subscription, building trust and excitement for the future boxes to come.

Unboxing and experiencing a subscription box for the first time is a delightful moment that allows us to escape from the daily grind and indulge in something special. The surprises within the box bring a sense of joy and rejuvenation, reminding us that we deserve a little treat amidst our busy lives. As employees in the e-commerce niche, we understand the power of curated experiences, and subscription boxes provide just that – a monthly delight that is personalized to our interests and delivered to our doorstep.

In conclusion, unboxing and first impressions are integral to the subscription box experience. As employees in the e-commerce industry, we can truly appreciate the convenience and joy that these boxes bring. So go ahead, treat yourself to the ultimate surprise and discover the perfect monthly treats that will make you feel valued and appreciated in your busy life.

Trying and Testing the Products

As employees in the fast-paced world of e-commerce, we understand the importance of finding ways to treat ourselves amidst the daily hustle and bustle. That's where subscription boxes come in – the perfect monthly treats that can bring a little joy and excitement to our lives. But with so many options available, how do we know which ones are worth our hard-earned money? That's where trying and testing the products becomes crucial.

In this subchapter, we'll delve into the process of trying and testing subscription box products, ensuring that you make informed choices and get the most out of your monthly treats. Whether you're new to subscription boxes or a seasoned enthusiast, these tips and tricks will help you navigate the vast sea of options available, ensuring that you find the perfect fit for your preferences.

First and foremost, we'll discuss the importance of research before committing to a subscription box. With numerous niches within the e-commerce industry, it's essential to identify your specific interests and needs. Are you a beauty enthusiast, a foodie, or perhaps a fitness fanatic? Understanding your preferences will help narrow down the options and increase the likelihood of finding a subscription box that aligns with your passions.

Once you've identified your niche, it's time for the fun part – trying and testing the products. It's crucial to make the most of each item in your subscription box to truly evaluate its value. Take the time to thoroughly examine and use each product, paying attention to quality, functionality, and overall satisfaction. Keep notes on your experiences, as this will help you compare different subscription boxes and provide valuable feedback for future purchases.

Another important aspect of trying and testing the products is engaging with the subscription box community. Join online forums, social media groups, and even attend local events to connect with fellow enthusiasts. By sharing your experiences and listening to others, you'll gain valuable insights and recommendations that can guide your subscription box journey.

Remember, trying and testing the products is not only about personal enjoyment but also about discovering new brands and supporting small businesses. By actively engaging with the products you receive, you're encouraging innovation and growth within the e-commerce industry.

In conclusion, trying and testing the products is an essential step in finding the perfect subscription box. By conducting thorough research, actively engaging with the products, and connecting with the subscription box community, you can ensure that your monthly treats bring you joy, excitement, and a true sense of fulfillment. So go ahead, delve into the world of subscription boxes, and unlock the perfect monthly treat for yourself – you deserve it!

Incorporating Subscription Box Items into Your Daily Routine

Subscription boxes have become the latest trend in the e-commerce industry, offering a convenient and exciting way to discover new products and treats. As busy employees, it can be challenging to find the time to explore new items and incorporate them into our daily lives. However, with a little planning and creativity, you can make the most out of your subscription box items and enhance your daily routine.

One of the advantages of subscription boxes is the element of surprise they bring. Each month, you receive a curated selection of products that cater to your specific interests and needs. To fully capitalize on this, take some time to research the items you receive. Whether it's beauty products, snacks, or office supplies, understanding the benefits and features of each item will help you make the most informed decisions on how to incorporate them into your routine.

For example, if your subscription box includes a new skincare product, take the time to learn about its ingredients and benefits. Then, incorporate it into your daily skincare routine, perhaps as a morning or evening ritual. By doing so, not only will you use the product regularly, but you will also enjoy the full benefits it offers.

Another way to incorporate subscription box items into your daily routine is by thinking outside the box. Don't limit yourself to the intended purpose of each item; instead, explore creative ways to use them. For instance, if you receive a healthy snack in your box, consider using it as an alternative to your regular mid-afternoon junk food. This way, you can enjoy a delicious treat while also fueling your body with nutritious ingredients.

Furthermore, subscription boxes often include items that can enhance your workspace or improve your productivity. If you receive office supplies or gadgets, find ways to integrate them into your daily work routine. Whether it's a stylish pen, a desk organizer, or a time management tool, these items can elevate your workspace and make your workday more enjoyable and efficient.

Incorporating subscription box items into your daily routine is not only about using the products but also about embracing the element of surprise and discovery. Take the time to explore and experiment with each item, and you may find hidden gems that become essential parts of your daily life. With a little creativity and planning, subscription boxes can truly be the perfect monthly treat for busy employees in the e-commerce industry.

Sharing and Collaborating with Other Subscribers

In today's fast-paced world, subscription boxes have taken the e-commerce industry by storm, offering busy employees a convenient and exciting way to discover new products. However, the benefits of subscription boxes extend beyond the individual experience. One of the most enjoyable aspects of subscribing to a monthly treat is the opportunity to share and collaborate with other subscribers, making the experience even more rewarding.

Sharing your subscription box goodies with colleagues or friends can create a sense of camaraderie and foster a shared excitement for new discoveries. Whether it's a box filled with snacks, beauty products, or even books, there's nothing quite like unboxing with others and witnessing their genuine joy. By sharing the experience, you can engage in meaningful conversations, swap items, and even bond over common interests. It's a fantastic way to build connections and create a positive atmosphere in your workplace or social circle.

Collaborating with other subscribers takes the sharing experience to another level. Many subscription box services provide online platforms, forums, or social media groups where subscribers can connect and collaborate. These platforms allow you to exchange feedback, share tips and tricks, and even suggest new products or themes. It's an excellent opportunity to tap into the collective wisdom and experiences of a diverse group of individuals who share your interests.

Moreover, collaborating with other subscribers can lead to exciting partnerships or joint ventures. Perhaps you find someone who shares your passion for healthy snacks and wants to start a blog together, or maybe you discover a fellow bookworm who would be a great reading buddy. The possibilities are endless when you connect with like-minded individuals through your subscription box community.

Remember, sharing and collaborating with other subscribers doesn't have to be limited to your immediate circle. Engaging with the wider subscriber community can provide inspiration, support, and a sense of belonging. By actively participating in discussions, attending meet-ups or virtual events, and following influencers or ambassadors associated with your subscription box, you can expand your network and enhance your overall experience.

In conclusion, subscription boxes not only offer a personalized monthly treat for busy employees in the e-commerce industry, but they also provide an opportunity to share and collaborate with other subscribers. By sharing your unboxing experience with colleagues or friends, you can foster connections and create a positive atmosphere in your workplace or social circle. Collaborating with other subscribers through online platforms and forums allows you to tap into a collective wealth of knowledge, exchange feedback, and potentially form partnerships or joint ventures. So, don't hesitate to embrace the social aspect of subscription boxes and immerse yourself in the vibrant community of like-minded individuals.

Providing Feedback and Reviews

As employees in the fast-paced world of e-commerce, it is important to understand the significance of providing feedback and reviews. In this subchapter, we will explore the power of your voice in shaping the subscription box industry and how your feedback can contribute to the success of e-commerce businesses.

Subscription box services have gained immense popularity in recent years, offering a convenient and personalized way to discover new products. As employees in the e-commerce industry, you have firsthand experience with these monthly treats and can provide invaluable feedback to both the subscription box companies and fellow consumers.

Your feedback serves as a crucial tool for subscription box companies to understand what works and what doesn't. By sharing your thoughts, you help these businesses improve their offerings, ensuring that the products and experiences provided align with your expectations. Your insights can help shape the development of future boxes, leading to a better overall experience for all subscribers.

When providing feedback, be specific and constructive. Highlight what you liked about the products, as well as any areas for improvement. Remember, your feedback is not only beneficial to the companies but also to potential customers who rely on honest reviews to make informed decisions. By providing thoughtful reviews, you contribute to creating a transparent and trustworthy e-commerce community.

Additionally, your feedback can influence the growth and success of subscription box businesses. Positive reviews and recommendations can attract new customers, helping these companies expand their reach and thrive in the competitive e-commerce landscape. Your voice can make a significant impact on the success of these businesses, ultimately driving innovation and ensuring the continued availability of exciting subscription box options.

To maximize the impact of your feedback, consider joining online communities and platforms dedicated to subscription box reviews. These forums allow you to connect with fellow subscribers, exchange opinions, and discover new boxes. By actively participating in these communities, you not only enhance your own subscription box experience but also contribute to the growth of the e-commerce industry.

In conclusion, providing feedback and reviews is an essential part of being an employee in the e-commerce industry. Your opinions and insights play a significant role in shaping the subscription box industry and ensuring the satisfaction of both subscribers and businesses. So, take the time to share your thoughts, make your voice heard, and help create a thriving e-commerce community built on transparency and consumer empowerment.

Chapter 5: Managing Your Subscription Box Subscriptions

Tracking and Organizing Your Deliveries

In the fast-paced world of e-commerce, subscription boxes have become a popular way for busy employees to receive their favorite treats conveniently at their doorstep every month. However, with multiple subscriptions, tracking and organizing your deliveries can sometimes be a daunting task. But worry not! In this subchapter, we will guide you on how to efficiently track and organize your deliveries, ensuring a hassle-free experience.

First and foremost, consider creating a dedicated email address solely for your subscription boxes. This will help you keep track of all your subscription-related emails in one place, making it easier to manage and stay organized. Set up filters and labels to categorize emails from different subscription services, allowing you to quickly identify and locate important information.

Next, leverage technology and download a delivery tracking app on your smartphone. These apps provide real-time updates on the status of your deliveries, allowing you to know exactly when your box will arrive. You can also opt-in for notifications, so you never miss a delivery or have to worry about package theft. With just a few taps, you can effortlessly track all your subscriptions in one convenient location.

Another effective way to stay organized is by creating a physical tracking system. Designate a specific area in your home or office to keep track of your subscription boxes. Use a whiteboard or a bulletin board to write down the expected delivery dates, tracking numbers, and any other relevant details. This visual reminder will help you keep track of your subscriptions, ensuring you don't miss out on any surprises or lose track of a delivery.

Furthermore, consider using a calendar app or an online calendar service to schedule reminders for your subscription box deliveries. Set up alerts a couple of days before the expected arrival date to ensure you're prepared and excited for the surprise. This will also help you manage your expectations and plan accordingly.

Lastly, don't forget to regularly evaluate your subscriptions. As an employee with a busy schedule, your preferences and needs may change over time. Take the time to assess whether your current subscriptions still align with your interests and budget. Consider canceling or changing subscriptions that no longer bring you joy or value.

By implementing these tracking and organizing strategies, you can effortlessly manage your subscription boxes and ensure that each monthly treat brings you delight and convenience. Stay organized, stay notified, and enjoy the ultimate subscription box experience designed specifically for busy employees like you in the e-commerce niche.

Dealing with Duplicate or Unwanted Items

As an employee who loves subscription boxes, there's nothing more exciting than receiving a monthly treat filled with surprises and goodies. However, there may come a time when you find yourself faced with duplicate or unwanted items. Don't worry – we've got you covered! In this subchapter, we will explore some effective strategies for dealing with duplicate or unwanted items in your subscription boxes.

1. Re-Gift or Donate: If you receive duplicate items that you don't necessarily need, consider re-gifting them to someone who would appreciate them. It could be a friend, family member, or colleague. Alternatively, you can donate them to a local charity or shelter. By doing so, you not only declutter your space but also spread joy to others.

2. Swap with Fellow Subscribers: Many subscription box enthusiasts participate in online communities or forums where they can connect with fellow subscribers. These platforms often have dedicated sections for swapping or trading items. If you have unwanted items, you can find someone who is willing to exchange them for something you desire. It's a win-win situation for everyone involved!

3. Sell or Trade: Another option is to sell your unwanted items. Online marketplaces, such as eBay or Facebook Marketplace, provide a convenient way to sell items you no longer want. Additionally, some subscription box companies offer buy/sell/trade groups on social media platforms, allowing subscribers to connect and trade items within the community.

4. Provide Feedback to the Subscription Box Company: If you consistently receive unwanted or duplicate items, it's essential to provide feedback to the subscription box company. They value customer opinions and want to ensure that subscribers are satisfied. By letting them know your preferences or concerns, they can make adjustments to improve future boxes.

5. Customize Your Box: Some subscription box services offer customization options, allowing you to choose the items you receive. If you consistently receive unwanted items, consider switching to a subscription box service that provides customization features. This way, you have more control over the items you receive and can avoid duplicates or unwanted items.

Remember, the goal of subscription boxes is to bring joy and excitement into your life. By implementing these strategies, you can effectively deal with duplicate or unwanted items and enhance your subscription box experience. Happy unboxing!

Pausing or Cancelling Subscriptions

In today's fast-paced world, subscription boxes have become a popular trend, offering convenience and excitement right at your doorstep. As an employee navigating the e-commerce landscape, it's essential to understand how to manage your subscriptions effectively. While these monthly treats can bring joy and surprise to your life, there may come a time when you need to pause or cancel your subscriptions temporarily or permanently. This subchapter will guide you through the process, ensuring you have the knowledge to make informed decisions about your subscription boxes.

Pausing a subscription is a great option when you anticipate a busy period or when you want to take a break from receiving monthly treats. Most e-commerce subscription services offer this feature to accommodate their customers' needs. By pausing your subscription, you can temporarily halt deliveries without losing any benefits or rewards associated with the service. Whether it's for a vacation, a hectic work schedule, or simply wanting to try something new, pausing your subscription allows you to maintain flexibility without any long-term commitments.

On the other hand, there may be instances where cancelling your subscription becomes necessary. Life circumstances change, and your monthly treat might no longer suit your preferences or budget. Cancelling a subscription should be a straightforward process, but it's essential to understand the terms and conditions outlined by the e-commerce company. Some subscriptions require a notice period or have specific cancellation policies, while others offer a hassle-free cancellation process. It's crucial to familiarize yourself with these details to ensure a smooth experience.

When considering cancelling a subscription, take a moment to reflect on why you're doing so. Maybe it's time to explore new interests or try a different subscription box that aligns better with your current needs. Don't hesitate to reach out to customer support or browse through customer reviews to gather insights and make an informed decision. Remember, the subscription box industry is vast, and there's always a perfect fit for every employee.

In conclusion, managing your subscription boxes effectively is key to maximizing the joy and benefits they bring. Whether you need to pause your subscription temporarily or cancel it permanently, understanding the process and your options is crucial. By taking the time to assess your needs and exploring different subscription box options, you can ensure a delightful monthly treat experience tailored to your preferences as a busy employee in the e-commerce world.

Exploring Special Edition and Limited-Time Boxes

In the ever-evolving world of e-commerce, subscription boxes have taken the market by storm, offering a convenient and exciting way for busy employees to pamper themselves. These monthly treats not only add a touch of delight to their lives but also provide an escape from the daily grind. One of the most enticing aspects of subscription boxes is the availability of special edition and limited-time boxes that cater to specific themes, events, or seasons.

Special edition boxes are an exceptional way to experience something unique and extraordinary. They are carefully curated to align with a particular occasion, such as holidays, anniversaries, or collaborations with renowned brands. These boxes often feature exclusive products, limited-edition items, or even personalized surprises that cannot be found elsewhere. Whether it's a Valentine's Day box filled with romantic goodies, a Halloween box packed with spooky treats, or a box celebrating a popular movie release, special edition boxes offer an element of surprise and anticipation that regular monthly boxes may not provide.

Limited-time boxes, on the other hand, are designed to create a sense of urgency and exclusivity. These boxes are available for a short period, usually just a few days or weeks, and once they're gone, they're gone. Limited-time boxes often boast a unique assortment of products or collaborations with influencers, making them highly sought after by eager subscribers. These boxes may focus on a specific niche, such as beauty, fitness, or self-care, allowing employees to indulge in their passions or discover new interests.

Exploring special edition and limited-time boxes not only adds excitement to your subscription box journey but also enables you to stay up-to-date with the latest trends and exclusive offerings. With each box you receive, you'll unwrap a new experience and have a chance to try products that may not have been otherwise accessible. It's like receiving a personalized gift tailored to your interests, delivered right to your doorstep.

As an employee seeking a monthly treat that perfectly complements your busy lifestyle, special edition and limited-time boxes are a fantastic way to elevate your subscription box experience. So, keep an eye out for these extraordinary offerings and be prepared to be pleasantly surprised when you unbox your next monthly treasure.

Navigating Subscription Box Marketplaces and Aggregators

In today's fast-paced world, where time is a precious commodity, subscription boxes have emerged as a convenient and exciting solution for busy employees. These monthly treats bring joy and surprise right to your doorstep, offering a curated selection of products tailored to your interests. As employees in the e-commerce industry, it's essential to make informed choices when exploring subscription box marketplaces and aggregators. This subchapter will guide you through the process, ensuring you find the perfect monthly subscription box.

Subscription box marketplaces act as a hub, connecting customers with a wide range of box options. These platforms offer a variety of niches, from beauty and wellness to food and gaming. As an employee in the e-commerce sector, you have the advantage of understanding market dynamics and evaluating the viability of different subscription box businesses. Take advantage of this knowledge by exploring marketplaces that allow you to browse and compare options side by side. Look for platforms that provide detailed information, such as customer reviews, product descriptions, and pricing details, to make an informed decision.

Aggregators are another valuable tool that simplifies the subscription box discovery process. These platforms aggregate boxes across multiple marketplaces, allowing you to explore a vast selection without visiting each individual website. By leveraging aggregator platforms, you save time and effort while gaining access to a broader range of subscription box options. Keep in mind that not all aggregators cover every marketplace, so it's essential to explore multiple sources to ensure you don't miss out on unique and niche offerings.

When navigating subscription box marketplaces and aggregators, it's crucial to consider a few key factors. First, identify your interests and preferences. Are you passionate about skincare, wellness, or gourmet food? Understanding your preferences will help you narrow down your search and find a subscription box that aligns with your interests. Additionally, consider your budget. Subscription box prices vary widely, so it's crucial to set a realistic spending limit to avoid overspending.

As an employee in the e-commerce industry, you possess the knowledge and skills to evaluate the quality and value of products. Utilize this expertise by thoroughly researching each subscription box's contents, ensuring they meet your expectations. Look for transparency and quality assurance from the companies, as well as positive customer feedback.

By navigating subscription box marketplaces and aggregators with these considerations in mind, you'll discover the perfect monthly treat that brings joy and excitement to your busy life. Stay tuned for the next chapter, where we delve into the best practices for choosing the ideal subscription box for your needs and preferences.

Chapter 6: Exploring Subscription Box Alternatives

Renting and Borrowing Services

In today's world of e-commerce, where convenience and flexibility are paramount, the concept of renting and borrowing services has gained immense popularity. For busy employees who are always on the go, these services offer a convenient and cost-effective way to access the products they need, without the burden of ownership. Whether it's clothing, accessories, home appliances, or even cars, renting and borrowing services have revolutionized the way we consume.

One of the key advantages of renting and borrowing services is the ability to try out different products and experiences without making a long-term commitment. For employees who are constantly seeking new and innovative ways to enhance their lives, this flexibility is a game-changer. Need a new outfit for a special occasion? Instead of spending a fortune on buying a dress that will only be worn once, you can simply rent a stunning designer piece for a fraction of the cost. Similarly, if you're planning a weekend getaway and require a car, why not borrow one from a car-sharing service instead of investing in an expensive vehicle? These services not only save you money but also give you the freedom to explore different options without the hassle of maintenance and storage.

Renting and borrowing services also align with the growing trend of sustainability and conscious consumerism. By opting for these services, employees can reduce their carbon footprint by minimizing waste and unnecessary consumption. Rather than contributing to the cycle of constant buying and discarding, renting and borrowing encourage a more mindful approach to consumption.

Moreover, renting and borrowing services cater to the diverse needs of employees by offering a wide range of products and experiences. Whether you're a fashion enthusiast, a tech junkie, or a fitness fanatic, there is a subscription box or rental service tailored to your niche. These services often provide curated selections, personalized recommendations, and the convenience of doorstep delivery, making them a perfect fit for busy employees who value time and convenience.

In conclusion, renting and borrowing services have revolutionized the way employees shop and consume products. With their flexibility, cost-effectiveness, and sustainability, these services offer a unique and convenient alternative to traditional ownership. By embracing the concept of renting and borrowing, employees can enhance their lives, explore new experiences, and contribute to a more sustainable future. So why commit to ownership when you can simply borrow or rent? Embrace the trend and discover the perfect monthly treats for your busy lifestyle.

Personalized Subscription Box Services

In the fast-paced world of e-commerce, subscription box services have gained immense popularity among busy employees. These services offer a convenient and personalized way to discover new products and indulge in monthly treats without the hassle of shopping. In this subchapter, we will explore the concept of personalized subscription box services and how they can cater to the needs and preferences of employees in the e-commerce industry.

Personalized subscription box services are designed to provide a unique and tailored experience for each subscriber. These services typically begin with a detailed questionnaire that helps the company understand the subscriber's preferences, interests, and lifestyle. Based on the information provided, the company curates a selection of products that are specifically chosen to match the subscriber's individual tastes and needs.

For employees in the e-commerce industry, personalized subscription box services offer a much-needed break from their hectic schedules. These boxes are carefully curated to include a variety of products that cater to different aspects of their lives. From self-care items to tech gadgets, healthy snacks to office supplies, each box is thoughtfully designed to enhance the subscriber's overall well-being and productivity.

What sets personalized subscription box services apart from traditional shopping is the element of surprise and discovery. Instead of spending hours browsing online stores, employees can look forward to receiving a curated package of hand-picked products every month. This not only saves time but also introduces them to new brands and products they may have never discovered otherwise.

Moreover, personalized subscription box services foster a sense of community among employees in the e-commerce industry. Many subscription box companies organize online forums or social media groups where subscribers can connect, share their experiences, and provide feedback. This creates a supportive network where employees can exchange recommendations, discuss their favorite products, and even collaborate on new ventures.

In conclusion, personalized subscription box services have revolutionized the way employees in the e-commerce industry discover and enjoy new products. By offering a customized selection of treats and essentials, these services provide a convenient and personalized shopping experience. From saving time and effort to fostering a sense of community, personalized subscription box services cater to the needs and preferences of busy employees in the e-commerce niche.

DIY and Craft Subscription Boxes

In today's fast-paced world, finding time to unwind and engage in creative activities can be a challenge for busy employees. However, with the rise of e-commerce, there is now an exciting solution that allows you to have an artistic escape delivered right to your doorstep – DIY and craft subscription boxes! These innovative services offer a wide range of projects and materials to help you explore your creative side and enjoy some much-needed relaxation.

DIY and craft subscription boxes are a great way to indulge in your hobbies without the hassle of sourcing materials or brainstorming project ideas. Each month, you will receive a curated box filled with all the necessary supplies, instructions, and inspiration to complete a unique craft project. Whether you're into painting, knitting, jewelry-making, or even candle-making, there is a subscription box tailored to your specific interests.

One of the major advantages of these subscription boxes is their convenience. As busy employees, time is of the essence, and these boxes provide you with everything you need to get started immediately. No more searching through multiple stores or spending hours online trying to find the right materials – it's all conveniently packaged and delivered right to your door. This ensures that you have more time to focus on the creative process itself, allowing you to fully immerse yourself in the joy of crafting.

Furthermore, DIY and craft subscription boxes offer a sense of community and connection. Many of these services have online communities and forums where subscribers can share their finished projects, seek advice, and connect with like-minded individuals. Engaging with others who share your passion for crafting can be inspiring and motivating, and it's a wonderful way to expand your network while honing your creative skills.

Additionally, these subscription boxes provide an excellent opportunity to explore new crafts and techniques. With each month's delivery, you'll be introduced to innovative projects that challenge your creativity and broaden your artistic horizons. From learning new painting techniques to mastering intricate embroidery patterns, these boxes allow you to continuously develop your skills and discover hidden talents.

In conclusion, DIY and craft subscription boxes offer a delightful escape for busy employees in the e-commerce industry. They provide convenience, community, and endless creative possibilities, making them the perfect monthly treat for those looking to unwind, relax, and indulge in their favorite hobbies. So why not treat yourself to a subscription box and unlock a world of artistic inspiration?

Local and Regional Subscription Box Services

As the popularity of subscription box services continues to rise, more and more companies are emerging to cater to niche markets and provide unique and personalized experiences for customers. One such category is local and regional subscription box services, which offer a delightful twist to the traditional monthly treat. These services focus on bringing the best products from local businesses right to your doorstep, supporting and promoting the local economy while providing you with a curated selection of goodies.

For employees who are passionate about supporting small businesses and discovering hidden gems in their local communities, local and regional subscription box services are the perfect fit. These boxes can include anything from artisanal food products and locally sourced ingredients to handcrafted accessories and unique home decor items. By subscribing to these services, employees not only get to enjoy high-quality, locally made products but also contribute to the growth and sustainability of their community.

One of the key advantages of local and regional subscription boxes is the element of surprise they bring to your monthly routine. Each month, you'll receive a carefully curated selection of products from different local businesses, allowing you to discover new favorites and indulge in a variety of treats. Whether it's a delicious homemade jam, a luxurious soap made with organic ingredients, or a beautifully designed piece of jewelry, these boxes are designed to bring joy and excitement to your doorstep.

Moreover, local and regional subscription box services often provide a unique opportunity for employees to connect with their community on a deeper level. By supporting local businesses and artisans, subscribers become part of a larger network of like-minded individuals who share a passion for quality, craftsmanship, and supporting the local economy. Many of these services also provide the opportunity to attend exclusive events, workshops, or tastings, allowing subscribers to engage directly with the makers and creators behind the products they receive.

In conclusion, local and regional subscription box services offer a delightful and meaningful way for employees to support their local community while enjoying the best products their region has to offer. By subscribing to these services, employees can indulge in the joy of discovery, connect with like-minded individuals, and contribute to the growth and sustainability of their local economy. So, if you're looking to add a touch of local flavor to your monthly treats, consider giving a local or regional subscription box service a try - you won't be disappointed!

Subscription Box Gift Options for Employees

In today's fast-paced world, finding the perfect gift for your hardworking employees can be a challenge. You want to show your appreciation for their dedication and commitment, but how do you find a gift that is unique, thoughtful, and suits their individual tastes and preferences? Look no further than subscription box gifts – the ultimate solution for busy employees in the e-commerce industry!

Subscription boxes have gained immense popularity in recent years, and for good reason. They offer a monthly treat that is carefully curated to cater to specific interests, making them the ideal gift for employees who deserve a little something extra. Whether it's a book lover, a foodie, a fitness enthusiast, or a fashionista, there is a subscription box out there tailored to their niche.

For the e-commerce industry, where employees are constantly immersed in the world of online shopping, a subscription box can be a delightful surprise that adds a touch of excitement to their daily routine. Imagine receiving a box filled with the latest gadgets, trendy accessories, or exclusive discounts on e-commerce platforms – it's like Christmas every month!

One popular subscription box option for e-commerce employees is the "Tech Box," which includes cutting-edge gadgets, tech accessories, and innovative products. It keeps them up-to-date with the latest tech trends and enhances their productivity in the digital world. Another great option is the "Fashion Box," which delivers curated clothing items, accessories, and styling tips, helping employees stay fashionable and confident in their professional lives.

For the health-conscious employees, a "Fitness Box" can be a perfect choice. Packed with workout gear, healthy snacks, and personalized fitness plans, it encourages them to maintain an active lifestyle amidst their busy schedules. Similarly, a "Foodie Box" can bring joy to those who appreciate culinary delights, with gourmet ingredients, unique recipes, and artisanal treats delivered right to their doorstep.

By gifting subscription boxes to your employees, you not only show your appreciation but also encourage self-care and personal growth. These monthly treats remind them to take a break, indulge in their hobbies, and explore new interests. It's the perfect way to say, "Thank you for your hard work, now take some time for yourself!"

In conclusion, subscription box gifts are a fantastic option for busy employees in the e-commerce industry. From tech enthusiasts to fashion lovers, fitness buffs to foodies, there is a subscription box tailored to every niche. By surprising your employees with these monthly treats, you motivate and reward them, while also promoting self-care and personal development. So why wait? Start exploring the world of subscription boxes and give your employees the perfect gift they truly deserve!

Chapter 7: Subscription Box Etiquette and Best Practices

Respecting Delivery and Shipping Guidelines

In the fast-paced world of e-commerce, timely delivery and efficient shipping are vital components for ensuring customer satisfaction. As an employee working in the e-commerce industry, understanding and respecting delivery and shipping guidelines is crucial for the success of your business. This subchapter aims to provide you with valuable insights and tips on how to navigate this aspect of your job effectively.

1. Importance of Timely Delivery: Timely delivery is the backbone of any successful e-commerce business. Customers expect their orders to arrive promptly, and any delays can result in negative reviews and a loss of trust. As an employee, it is essential to prioritize efficient order processing, packaging, and timely handover to shipping partners.

2. Understanding Shipping Guidelines: Shipping guidelines vary depending on the carrier, destination, and type of product being shipped. Familiarize yourself with your company's specific guidelines to ensure compliance. This includes understanding packaging requirements, weight and size restrictions, and any special handling instructions.

3. Efficient Packaging: Proper packaging is essential to protect products during transit. Use sturdy materials and appropriate cushioning to prevent damage. Additionally, ensure that the packaging is compact and lightweight, as it can reduce shipping costs and minimize the environmental impact.

4.   Accurate   Documentation: Complete and accurate documentation is a critical aspect of shipping. Ensure that all necessary documents, such as customs forms or shipping labels, are correctly filled out to avoid delays or customs issues. Double-check the accuracy of recipient addresses to prevent delivery errors.

5.   Tracking   and   Communication: Tracking shipments is essential to keep customers informed about the status of their orders. Familiarize yourself with the tracking systems used by your company and be prepared to provide accurate information to customers when they inquire about their deliveries.

6.   Dealing   with   Shipping   Issues: Despite our best efforts, shipping issues can still arise. In the event of a delayed or lost shipment, promptly communicate with the customer and provide updates on the situation. Address their concerns and work towards finding a satisfactory resolution, which may include offering a refund, replacement, or alternative solution.

By respecting delivery and shipping guidelines, you contribute to the seamless functioning of your company's e-commerce operations. Efficient and timely delivery enhances customer satisfaction, fosters trust, and ultimately drives repeat business. Remember, as an employee in the e-commerce industry, you play a crucial role in ensuring that every customer receives their monthly treats promptly and in pristine condition.

Interacting with Subscription Box Companies and Customer Support

In the fast-paced world of e-commerce, subscription box companies have become a popular choice for busy employees looking for a monthly treat. These companies offer a wide range of products and services, from beauty and wellness to food and beverages, delivered right to your doorstep. However, like any other online purchase, it is essential to know how to interact with these companies and their customer support to ensure a smooth and satisfying experience.

When it comes to subscription box companies, communication is key. Before subscribing to a service, take the time to research the company's reputation and read customer reviews. Look for companies with responsive and helpful customer support teams, as they will be your go-to resource for any questions or concerns you may have throughout your subscription.

Once you have subscribed to a service, familiarize yourself with the company's policies and terms. This includes understanding the cancellation policy, delivery schedule, and any additional fees or charges that may apply. By being well-informed, you can avoid any surprises or misunderstandings down the line.

If you have a specific request or preference, such as dietary restrictions or product preferences, reach out to the company's customer support. Most subscription box companies are willing to accommodate their customers' needs and preferences, ensuring that you receive products that align with your interests and lifestyle.

Customer support is not just there to address issues or concerns; they can also provide valuable recommendations and suggestions. If you are unsure about a particular product or need guidance on how to make the most of your subscription, don't hesitate to reach out. They have a wealth of knowledge and experience and can help enhance your subscription box experience.

In the event that you encounter any issues or problems with your subscription box, contact customer support promptly. Be clear and concise about the problem and provide any necessary information, such as order numbers or account details. Most companies strive to resolve issues quickly and efficiently, ensuring customer satisfaction.

Interacting with subscription box companies and their customer support is an essential part of enjoying a seamless and rewarding experience. By being proactive, well-informed, and communicative, you can make the most out of your subscription box journey and discover the perfect monthly treats that suit your busy employee lifestyle.

Sharing and Promoting Subscription Box Discoveries

In today's fast-paced digital world, subscription boxes have become a popular trend in the e-commerce industry. These curated boxes offer a convenient and exciting way for busy employees to discover new products and experiences on a monthly basis. However, the subscription box experience doesn't end with just receiving the box. To truly maximize the value of your subscription, it's important to share and promote your discoveries.

Sharing your subscription box discoveries can have multiple benefits. Firstly, it allows you to spread the word about the amazing products you receive, contributing to the growth of the e-commerce brands you love. Additionally, sharing your experiences can create a sense of community among fellow employees who also subscribe to different boxes. It opens up opportunities for engaging conversations, recommendations, and even potential collaborations.

Social media platforms provide the perfect avenue for sharing your subscription box discoveries. Instagram, for instance, allows you to visually showcase the products and share your thoughts through captivating captions. By using relevant hashtags, you can connect with other enthusiasts and potentially gain new followers who share similar interests. Facebook groups and online forums dedicated to subscription boxes are also great places to share your experiences and connect with others.

When sharing your subscription box discoveries, it's important to be authentic and genuine. Focus on highlighting the products you truly enjoyed and explain why they stood out to you. People value honest opinions, so don't shy away from mentioning any drawbacks or areas for improvement. This transparency will not only benefit your fellow employees but also help e-commerce brands understand their customers' preferences and make necessary adjustments.

Promoting your subscription box discoveries can go beyond social media. Consider writing reviews on blogs or leaving feedback on the brand's website. These actions not only help potential customers make informed decisions but also contribute to the growth and success of the e-commerce brands you support. Additionally, some subscription box services offer referral programs where you can earn rewards or discounts by referring others. Take advantage of these opportunities to share your love for subscription boxes and potentially save some money in the process!

In conclusion, sharing and promoting your subscription box discoveries can be a rewarding experience that extends beyond the products themselves. By engaging with others and spreading the word about the brands you love, you contribute to the growth of the e-commerce industry while creating a sense of community among fellow employees. So, don't hesitate to share your subscription box experiences and help others discover the perfect monthly treats too!

Engaging with Subscription Box Communities and Influencers

In the world of e-commerce, subscription boxes have become a popular trend, offering a convenient and exciting way for busy employees to discover new products and experiences on a monthly basis. As an employee interested in exploring the world of subscription boxes, engaging with the communities and influencers associated with this industry can significantly enhance your experience and help you make the most of your subscription box journey.

Subscription box communities are online platforms where subscribers and enthusiasts come together to share their experiences, recommendations, and feedback. These communities can be found on social media platforms, forums, and dedicated websites. By actively participating in these communities, you can connect with like-minded individuals who share your interests and learn from their experiences. You can ask questions, seek advice, and even share your own thoughts and discoveries. This engagement will not only enrich your subscription box experience but also help you build a network of individuals who can guide you through the vast array of subscription box options available.

In addition to engaging with communities, influencers play a significant role in the subscription box industry. Influencers are individuals who have established a strong online presence and have a dedicated following. They provide valuable insights, reviews, and unboxing experiences, helping you make informed decisions when choosing subscription boxes. Following and interacting with influencers in the subscription box niche can provide you with inspiration, recommendations, and exclusive promotions. Many influencers also collaborate with subscription box companies to curate their own boxes, which can offer a unique and personalized experience.

To actively engage with subscription box communities and influencers, start by identifying the platforms and influencers that resonate with your interests. Follow relevant social media accounts, join forums, and subscribe to newsletters or blogs. Regularly participate in discussions, share your experiences, and ask questions. Engaging with others in the community will not only enhance your knowledge but also allow you to contribute to the growth of the subscription box industry.

In conclusion, engaging with subscription box communities and influencers is crucial for employees interested in exploring the world of subscription boxes. By actively participating in communities and following influencers, you can gain valuable insights, recommendations, and exclusive promotions. This engagement will not only enhance your subscription box experience but also allow you to build a network of like-minded individuals who can guide you through your subscription box journey. So, embrace the power of community and influencers, and discover the perfect monthly treats for yourself as a busy employee.

Being Mindful of Sustainability and Environmental Impact

In recent years, the concept of sustainability and environmental impact has gained significant traction across various industries, including the booming e-commerce sector. As employees in the e-commerce niche, it is crucial for us to understand the importance of being mindful of sustainability and the environmental impact our actions can have. This subchapter will delve into the significance of adopting sustainable practices in the e-commerce industry and how we, as employees, can contribute to a greener future.

The e-commerce industry has revolutionized the way we shop, providing convenience and access to a wide range of products at our fingertips. However, this convenience often comes at a cost to the environment. The packaging waste generated by e-commerce operations, along with the carbon emissions from transportation, are significant contributors to environmental degradation. As employees working in this industry, it is our responsibility to actively seek ways to minimize these impacts.

One effective way to address sustainability concerns is by embracing eco-friendly packaging solutions. By opting for recycled or biodegradable packaging materials, we can significantly reduce the amount of waste generated. Additionally, encouraging customers to recycle or reuse packaging materials can further contribute to sustainable practices.

Another aspect to consider is the transportation and logistics involved in e-commerce operations. As employees, we can explore greener alternatives, such as optimizing delivery routes to reduce fuel consumption or utilizing electric vehicles for transportation. These small changes can have a substantial positive impact on the environment.

Furthermore, it is important to be mindful of the products we offer through our e-commerce platforms. Prioritizing sustainable and ethically sourced products can help promote a greener and more conscious consumer culture. By vetting suppliers and supporting environmentally friendly brands, we can align our business practices with our commitment to sustainability.

In conclusion, being mindful of sustainability and environmental impact is crucial for employees in the e-commerce industry. By adopting eco-friendly packaging solutions, optimizing transportation methods, and prioritizing sustainable products, we can contribute to a greener future. As individuals, we have the power to make a difference and shape the e-commerce industry in a way that is more environmentally conscious. Let us strive to create a sustainable and thriving e-commerce ecosystem that not only benefits our businesses but also supports a healthier planet.

Chapter 8: Future Trends and Innovations in Subscription Boxes

Technology Integration and Personalization

In today's fast-paced world, technology integration has become an integral part of almost every aspect of our lives. From ordering groceries online to streaming our favorite movies, technology has made our lives more convenient and efficient. The e-commerce industry is no exception to this trend, as it has revolutionized the way we shop and consume products. In this subchapter, we will explore the concept of technology integration and its role in personalizing the e-commerce experience for busy employees.

Technology integration refers to the seamless incorporation of technology into various processes and systems. In the context of e-commerce, it involves using technology to enhance customer experiences and streamline operations. One of the key benefits of technology integration is personalization, which allows companies to tailor their offerings to individual preferences and needs.

Personalization is crucial in the e-commerce industry, especially for busy employees who often have limited time to shop. By leveraging technology, companies can gather data on customers' past purchases, browsing history, and preferences to provide personalized recommendations. For example, an e-commerce platform can use machine learning algorithms to analyze a customer's purchase history and suggest products that align with their interests. This level of personalization not only saves time for busy employees but also enhances their overall shopping experience.

Moreover, technology integration enables companies to offer a wide range of customization options. Whether it's selecting specific products, choosing delivery dates, or customizing packaging, employees can personalize their subscription box experience according to their preferences. This level of customization fosters a sense of exclusivity and ensures that employees receive products that genuinely resonate with their tastes and interests.

Additionally, technology integration allows for efficient inventory management and order fulfillment. By leveraging automated systems and advanced analytics, e-commerce companies can optimize their supply chain, ensuring that products are always in stock and delivered on time. This seamless process not only improves customer satisfaction but also reduces the chances of employees receiving products that do not meet their expectations.

In conclusion, technology integration plays a significant role in personalizing the e-commerce experience for busy employees. By leveraging technology, companies can provide personal recommendations, offer customization options, and streamline operations. This ultimately leads to a more convenient and tailored shopping experience, allowing employees to enjoy the perfect monthly treats without the hassle of traditional shopping methods.

Sustainability and Eco-Friendly Packaging

In today's world, where the impacts of climate change are becoming increasingly evident, it is more important than ever for businesses to prioritize sustainability and eco-friendly practices. As employees in the e-commerce industry, we have a unique opportunity to make a positive difference by embracing sustainable packaging options.

Sustainability is about meeting the needs of the present without compromising the ability of future generations to meet their own needs. When it comes to packaging, sustainability involves reducing waste, minimizing the use of harmful materials, and promoting recycling and reusability.

Eco-friendly packaging options have numerous benefits for both businesses and consumers. For businesses, sustainable packaging can help reduce costs associated with materials, transportation, and waste management. By opting for eco-friendly materials, such as biodegradable or compostable alternatives, e-commerce companies can enhance their brand image and attract environmentally conscious customers. Moreover, sustainable packaging can also contribute to regulatory compliance and help businesses meet their corporate social responsibility goals.

For consumers, receiving products in sustainable packaging can foster a sense of satisfaction and align with their values. Eco-friendly packaging also provides an opportunity for businesses to educate customers about the importance of sustainability and encourage them to make conscious choices.

There are several options available for e-commerce companies looking to adopt sustainable packaging practices. One approach is to use recycled materials for packaging, such as cardboard boxes made from post-consumer waste. Another option is to explore biodegradable or compostable packaging materials, which can break down naturally without harming the environment. Additionally, businesses can also consider using minimal packaging or opting for reusable packaging solutions, like cloth bags or boxes that can be returned and reused.

Implementing sustainable packaging practices may require some initial investment, but the long-term benefits far outweigh the costs. By reducing waste, minimizing environmental impacts, and appealing to eco-conscious consumers, e-commerce businesses can enhance their reputation, attract new customers, and contribute to a greener future.

As employees in the e-commerce industry, let us take the lead in promoting sustainability and eco-friendly practices. By making thoughtful choices regarding packaging, we can make a significant impact on the environment and inspire others to join the movement towards a more sustainable future.

Influencer and Celebrity Collaborations

One of the key strategies that e-commerce subscription box companies have used to skyrocket their success is partnering with influencers and celebrities. This chapter explores the power of influencer and celebrity collaborations and how they can benefit both the subscription box company and busy employees like you.

In today's digital age, influencers have become the new celebrities, with their massive online followings and ability to sway consumer behavior. By teaming up with influencers who align with their brand values, subscription box companies can tap into a highly engaged audience and gain exposure to a whole new customer base.

For employees, this means access to exclusive collaborations and partnerships that bring added value to their subscription box experience. Imagine receiving a box curated by your favorite lifestyle influencer or endorsed by a celebrity you admire. These collaborations not only add excitement to your monthly treat but also provide an opportunity to discover new products and brands that align with your interests and values.

By leveraging influencer and celebrity partnerships, e-commerce subscription box companies can also enhance the overall customer experience. These collaborations often come with special promotions, discounts, or unique products that are only available through the subscription box. This gives employees an extra sense of exclusivity and a chance to try out products or services they may not have discovered otherwise.

Additionally, influencer and celebrity collaborations can serve as a trust-building mechanism for busy employees who may be hesitant to try new products or services. When a well-known personality endorses a subscription box, it lends credibility to the company and the products they offer. This reassurance can help employees feel more confident in their purchasing decisions, making the subscription box experience even more enjoyable.

In conclusion, influencer and celebrity collaborations have become a powerful tool in the e-commerce subscription box industry. By partnering with influencers and celebrities, subscription box companies can reach new audiences, offer exclusive collaborations, enhance the customer experience, and build trust with busy employees like you. So, get ready to be treated to extraordinary monthly surprises curated by your favorite influencers and celebrities in the world of e-commerce subscription boxes.

International Expansion and Global Subscription Box Market

In today's interconnected world, the opportunities for businesses to expand internationally are vast. The global subscription box market is no exception. As the e-commerce industry continues to thrive, the demand for subscription boxes across borders is rapidly increasing. This subchapter explores the potential of international expansion and the benefits it can bring to the global subscription box market.

E-commerce has revolutionized the way businesses operate, allowing them to reach customers around the globe. With the rise of online shopping, consumers have become more open to trying new products and experiences. Subscription boxes provide a unique opportunity for businesses to tap into this growing market. By expanding internationally, subscription box companies can gain access to a wider customer base and increase their revenue potential.

One of the key advantages of international expansion is the ability to diversify offerings. Different countries have their own unique cultures, preferences, and trends. By entering new markets, subscription box companies can tailor their products to meet the specific needs and interests of customers in each country. This customization not only enhances customer satisfaction but also opens up new revenue streams.

Moreover, entering international markets can also provide subscription box companies with a competitive edge. By expanding globally, businesses can establish themselves as pioneers in the industry and gain a first-mover advantage. This can help them build brand recognition and loyalty while staying ahead of their competitors.

However, expanding internationally does come with its own set of challenges. Cultural differences, language barriers, and logistical complexities are some of the hurdles that businesses must navigate. It is crucial for subscription box companies to conduct thorough market research and develop a solid international expansion strategy to ensure success.

To support international expansion efforts, various resources and platforms are available to subscription box companies. E-commerce platforms like Shopify and Amazon provide global reach and infrastructure, making it easier for businesses to sell their products across borders. Additionally, partnerships with local distributors or fulfillment centers can help overcome logistical challenges and ensure efficient delivery to international customers.

In conclusion, international expansion presents tremendous opportunities for the global subscription box market. By entering new markets, subscription box companies can diversify their offerings, gain a competitive advantage, and tap into the growing demand for curated monthly treats worldwide. While challenges exist, with the right strategy and resources, businesses can successfully expand internationally and thrive in the e-commerce industry.

Predictions for the Future of Subscription Boxes

As the e-commerce industry continues to evolve, subscription boxes have emerged as a popular trend among busy employees. These curated monthly treats offer convenience and surprise, catering to the unique needs and interests of individuals. With the increasing popularity of subscription boxes, it is essential for employees in the e-commerce niche to stay updated on the future trends and predictions in this industry.

1. Personalization: One of the key predictions for the future of subscription boxes is an increased emphasis on personalization. As technology advances, companies will be able to gather more data about their subscribers, allowing them to curate boxes that are tailored to individual preferences and needs. This level of personalization will enhance the overall subscriber experience and increase customer satisfaction.

2. Sustainability: With the rising concerns about the environment, subscription box companies are predicted to place a strong focus on sustainability in the coming years. This will involve using eco-friendly packaging materials, partnering with ethical and sustainable brands, and promoting recyclable or compostable products. Employees will witness a shift towards more conscious subscription box options that align with their values.

3. Integration of Augmented Reality (AR) and Virtual Reality (VR): In the future, subscription boxes may integrate AR and VR technology to enhance the unboxing experience. Subscribers will be able to virtually try on products, visualize how they fit into their lifestyle, or even participate in interactive games related to the box's theme. This

incorporation of immersive technologies will revolutionize the way employees engage with subscription boxes.

4. Expansion into niche markets: As the subscription box industry matures, companies will increasingly target niche markets to cater to specific interests and hobbies. Whether it's specialized boxes for fitness enthusiasts, bookworms, or crafters, employees can expect a wider range of subscription box options that cater to their unique passions.

5. Collaboration with Influencers: Influencer marketing has become a powerful tool for brands to reach their target audience. In the future, subscription box companies will collaborate with influencers to create exclusive boxes or offer customizations based on their recommendations. These partnerships will provide employees with curated boxes that reflect the latest trends and expert opinions.

In conclusion, the future of subscription boxes in the e-commerce industry looks promising for busy employees. With an increased focus on personalization, sustainability, integration of AR/VR, expansion into niches, and collaboration with influencers, employees can expect an even more exciting and tailored subscription box experience. By staying up to date with these predictions, employees can make informed choices while exploring the perfect monthly treats that cater to their busy lifestyles.

Chapter 9: Conclusion: Finding Your Perfect Monthly Treat

Reflecting on Your Subscription Box Journey

As busy employees in the fast-paced world of e-commerce, it's important to take a step back from time to time and reflect on the journey you've embarked upon with your subscription box. Whether you're a seasoned subscriber or just starting out, this subchapter is designed to help you gain a deeper understanding of the value your subscription brings to your life.

Subscription boxes have revolutionized the way we shop and indulge in our favorite products. They provide a convenient and exciting way to discover new items, pamper ourselves, and stay updated with the latest trends. Reflecting on your subscription box journey allows you to appreciate the positive impact it has had on your personal and professional life.

Firstly, take a moment to acknowledge the joy and excitement that comes with receiving your monthly treat. Remember the anticipation when your box arrives at your doorstep, the thrill of unboxing and uncovering the surprises inside. This simple pleasure can brighten up your day and bring a sense of delight even during the most hectic times.

Reflecting on your subscription box journey also encourages you to assess the value you're receiving from your subscription. Consider the convenience of having curated products delivered straight to your door, saving you time and effort in the process. Evaluate the quality and variety of items you've received and how they've enhanced your daily life or work routine. Take note of any products you've discovered and fallen in love with, as they may become staples in your life going forward.

Furthermore, reflecting on your subscription box journey can help you identify any areas for improvement or changes you'd like to make. Perhaps you've realized that you're not fully utilizing the products you receive, or maybe you're interested in exploring new types of subscription boxes that align better with your interests and needs. Use this reflection as an opportunity to tailor your subscription experience to your evolving preferences.

In conclusion, reflecting on your subscription box journey is an essential practice for busy employees in the e-commerce industry. It allows you to appreciate the joy and convenience your subscription brings, evaluate the value you're receiving, and identify any adjustments you want to make moving forward. Embrace this opportunity to make the most out of your subscription box experience and continue to discover the perfect monthly treats that make your busy life a little more enjoyable.

Continuing to Explore and Discover New Subscription Boxes

In the fast-paced world of e-commerce, subscription boxes have become a popular trend among employees looking for a monthly treat to brighten up their busy lives. These boxes offer a convenient and exciting way to discover new products and experiences tailored to your unique interests. The possibilities are endless, with subscription boxes available for everything from beauty and fashion to gourmet food and fitness.

One of the greatest advantages of subscription boxes is the element of surprise they bring. Each month, you can look forward to receiving a carefully curated selection of goodies, hand-picked by experts in the field. These experts have their finger on the pulse of the latest trends and innovations, ensuring you stay ahead of the curve.

If you're already a fan of subscription boxes, you may be wondering how to continue exploring and discovering new ones. The good news is that the market is constantly evolving, with new boxes being launched regularly. To stay up-to-date with the latest offerings, it's a good idea to join online communities and forums dedicated to subscription boxes. Here, you can connect with fellow enthusiasts who share their experiences and recommendations.

Another way to discover new subscription boxes is by attending trade shows and expos. These events bring together a wide range of vendors, allowing you to explore different niches and find boxes that align with your interests. You can interact with the creators, ask questions, and get a feel for the products before committing to a subscription.

Additionally, many subscription box companies offer limited-time collaborations or special edition boxes. These partnerships with well-known brands or influencers can introduce you to new and exciting products that may not be available elsewhere. Keep an eye out for these collaborations and be sure to act quickly, as they often sell out fast.

Lastly, don't be afraid to try something new! Stepping out of your comfort zone and exploring different niches can lead to delightful surprises. If you've always been into fashion and beauty boxes, why not give a food or wellness box a try? You never know what hidden gems you may discover.

In conclusion, as an employee in the e-commerce world, exploring and discovering new subscription boxes can add a touch of excitement and joy to your busy life. By staying engaged with online communities, attending trade shows, keeping an eye out for collaborations, and trying new niches, you'll ensure that your subscription box journey remains fresh and full of delightful surprises. So go ahead, indulge in the world of subscription boxes and let the monthly treats continue to bring joy to your doorstep!

Embracing the Joy of Monthly Surprises

In today's fast-paced world, where work-life balance feels like an elusive dream, finding time to treat yourself can be a real challenge. As busy employees in the e-commerce industry, your schedules are packed, leaving little room for self-care or enjoyable experiences. However, there is a solution that can bring excitement and joy back into your lives - subscription boxes!

Subscription boxes are a trend that has taken the e-commerce world by storm, offering a curated selection of products delivered right to your doorstep every month. These boxes are carefully designed to cater to various interests and preferences, ensuring that there is something for everyone. From beauty and skincare to gourmet snacks and books, the possibilities are endless.

Imagine the thrill of receiving a beautifully packaged box filled with surprises, tailored specifically to your tastes. Opening it up each month feels like unwrapping a personalized gift, providing a much-needed break from the monotony of work. Whether you are a foodie, a fashion enthusiast, or a wellness junkie, there is a subscription box out there waiting to delight you.

Not only do subscription boxes offer convenience and excitement, but they also provide an opportunity to discover new products and brands. With each box, you are introduced to a range of items carefully chosen by experts in the field. This exposure can help you stay up-to-date with the latest trends and innovations in your niche, allowing you to gain a competitive edge in the e-commerce industry.

Moreover, subscription boxes can be a valuable source of inspiration and motivation. As busy employees, it's easy to get caught up in the daily grind and lose sight of the things that bring us joy. These monthly treats serve as a reminder to take a moment for yourself, to indulge in something special, and to embrace the joy of surprises. They can rekindle your enthusiasm and inject a sense of fun into your routine, making work-life balance a little more attainable.

So, dear employees, it's time to embark on a journey of delightful surprises. Embrace the joy of subscription boxes and let them bring a monthly dose of happiness into your lives. Treat yourself and rediscover the pleasures that lie beyond your workplace. You deserve it!